Johannes Brahms

THREE ORCHESTRAL WORKS
IN FULL SCORE

Academic Festival Overture

Tragic Overture
and
Variations on a Theme
by Joseph Haydn

From the Breitkopf & Härtel Complete Works Edition

Edited by Hans Gál

DOVER PUBLICATIONS, INC.
New York

This Dover edition, first published in 1984, is an unabridged republica-
tion of Volume 3 (*Ouvertüren und Variationen für Orchester*) of *Johannes Brahms;
Sämtliche Werke; Ausgabe der Gesellschaft der Musikfreunde in Wien*, originally
published by Breitkopf & Härtel, Leipzig, n.d. (Editor's Commentary dated
Summer 1926). The Editor's Commentary was translated by Stanley Ap-
pelbaum specially for the present edition.

Library of Congress Cataloging in Publication Data
Brahms, Johannes, 1833-1899.
  [Orchestra music. Selections]
  Three orchestral works in full score.

  Reprint. Originally published: Leipzig : Breitkopf & Härtel, 1926?
(Sämtliche Werke / Johannes Brahms ; Bd. 3) With new English transla-
tion of the editorial commentary.
  Contents: Academic festival overture—Tragic overture—Variations on a
theme by Joseph Haydn.
  1. Overtures—Scores. 2. Variations (Orchestra)—Scores. I. Gál, Hans,
1890–   . II. Brahms, Johannes, 1833-1897. Akademische Festouvertüre.
1984. III. Brahms, Johannes, 1833-1897. Tragische Ouvertüre. 1984. IV.
Brahms, Johannes, 1833-1897. Variationen über ein Thema von Haydn. 1984.
V. Title. VI. Title: Orchestral works.
M1000.B73G3 1984   83-20559
ISBN-13: 978-0-486-24637-6
ISBN-10: 0-486-24637-X

Manufactured in the United States by LSC Communications
24637X16   2020
www.doverpublications.com

CONTENTS

EDITOR'S COMMENTARY

ACADEMIC FESTIVAL OVERTURE, OP. 80

SOURCE TEXTS:
1. Simrock's edition of the score.
2. Brahms's personal working copy of the printed score, in the possession of the Gesellschaft der Musikfreunde in Vienna.
3. The original MS, in the possession of the firm of N. Simrock, Berlin.

The overture, composed on the occasion of Brahms's honorary doctorate from the University of Breslau, was written in 1880 and published in 1881 with the title: "Akademische Festouvertüre für grosses Orchester von Johannes Brahms. Op. 80." Publication number 8187.

Brahms noted a few corrections in his working copy. These are certainly to be regarded as his final wishes and are therefore reflected in this edition. The original version of these passages is given below.

In the 4th measure after *A*, the Violas originally had a pizzicato *g* on the last quarter; Brahms replaced this with a quarter rest.

Correspondingly, four measures later, the Violas had a pizzicato *c* on the last quarter.

In the 2nd measure after *E*, Brahms extended a short crescendo mark for Violins 1 and 2 and Violas to the end of the following measure.

In the 13th measure after *F*, the Violins originally had *p dol. espress.* Brahms deleted the *espress.*, probably to avoid a premature swelling of volume.

Likewise, in the 17th measure after *M*, Brahms deleted an *espress.* for the Violins, and one for the Violas in the next measure.

A comparison with the original MS yielded nothing of significance for the editing of the text.

TRAGIC OVERTURE, OP. 81

SOURCE TEXTS:
1. Simrock's edition of the score.
2. Brahms's personal working copy of the printed score, in the possession of the Gesellschaft der Musikfreunde in Vienna.
3. The original MS, in the possession of the firm of N. Simrock, Berlin.

The overture was composed in 1880 and published in 1881 with the title: "Tragische Ouvertüre für Orchester von Johannes Brahms, Op. 81." Publication number 8189.

The printed score is virtually free of mistakes. Nor does Brahms's working copy contain any alterations. The original MS of the score shows only a few corrections, which pertain exclusively to dynamic markings.

VARIATIONS ON A THEME BY JOSEPH HAYDN, OP. 56a

SOURCE TEXTS:
1. Simrock's edition of the score (title: "Variationen über ein Thema von Jos. Haydn für Orchester von Johannes Brahms. Op. 56a"). Publication number 7395.
2. Brahms's personal working copy of the printed score, in the possession of the Gesellschaft der Musikfreunde in Vienna.
3. The original MS of the score, in the possession of the firm of N. Simrock, Berlin.

The Simrock score, published in 1874, is extremely correct apart from a few insignificant oversights. At the beginning of the 1st Variation, a *p* has been added here to the Kettledrums (by analogy with the other parts). In mm. 9 and 10 of the 3rd Variation, the original MS as well places the Bassoon notes a third too low (apparently a mistake in clef). It is worthy of mention that the Theme, as is clearly evident in the MS, was originally scored for strings. On the first page of the autograph MS is the indication: "If necessary, the Contrabassoon should be replaced by a Tuba (but only in the Thema and the Finale) according to the attached part."

VIENNA, SUMMER 1926   HANS GÁL

REVISIONSBERICHT

AKADEMISCHE FESTOUVERTÜRE
Op. 80.

VORLAGEN:

1. Die Simrocksche Druckausgabe der Partitur.
2. Brahms' Handexemplar, im Besitz der Gesellschaft der Musik-freunde in Wien.
3. Die Original-Handschrift, im Besitz des Verlags N. Simrock in Berlin.

Die Ouvertüre ist, durch Brahms' Ernennung zum Ehrendoktor durch die Breslauer Universität angeregt, im Jahre 1880 entstanden und erschien 1881 mit dem Titel: ›Akademische Festouvertüre für großes Orchester von Johannes Brahms. Op. 80.‹ Verlagsnummer 8187.

In Brahms' Handexemplar sind einige Korrekturen angemerkt, die jedenfalls als letztwillig zu betrachten sind und daher in dieser Ausgabe berücksichtigt wurden. Die ursprüngliche Fassung dieser Stellen ist nachstehend verzeichnet.

Im 4. Takt nach *A* stand ursprünglich in der Bratsche als letztes Viertel *g* pizzicato, von Brahms durch eine Viertelpause ersetzt.

Entsprechend lautete vier Takte später das letzte Viertel der Bratsche *c* pizzicato.

Im 2. Takt nach *E* hat Brahms ein kurzes Crescendo-Zeichen in 1. und 2. Violine und Bratsche bis zum Ende des folgenden Taktes verlängert.

Im 13. Takt nach *F* hatten die Violinen ursprünglich *p dol. es-press.* Das *espress.* ist gestrichen, wohl um ein vorzeitiges Crescendieren zu verhüten.

Ebenso ist im 17. Takt nach *M* ein *espress.* der Violinen, im folgenden Takt der Bratsche gestrichen.

Der Vergleich mit der Original-Handschrift ergab nichts für die Revision Bemerkenswertes.

Wien, im Sommer 1926.

TRAGISCHE OUVERTÜRE Op. 81.

VORLAGEN:

1. Die Simrocksche Druckausgabe der Partitur.
2. Brahms' Handexemplar, im Besitz der Gesellschaft der Musik-freunde in Wien.
3. Die Original-Handschrift, im Besitz des Verlags N. Simrock in Berlin.

Die Ouvertüre ist 1880 entstanden und erschien 1881 unter dem Titel: ›Tragische Ouvertüre für Orchester von Johannes Brahms. Op. 81.‹ Verlagsnummer 8189.

Die Partitur ist so gut wie fehlerfrei. Brahms' Handexemplar enthält auch keinerlei Richtigstellungen. Die Original-Handschrift der Partitur zeigt wenige Korrekturen, und diese fast ausschließlich in Hinsicht dynamischer Bezeichnungen.

VARIATIONEN ÜBER EIN THEMA VON HAYDN Op. 56 a.

VORLAGEN:

1. Die Simrocksche Partitur (Titel: Variationen über ein Thema von Jos. Haydn für Orchester von Johannes Brahms. Op. 56 a.) Verlagsnummer 7395.
2. Brahms' Handexemplar der Partitur, im Besitz der Gesellschaft der Musikfreunde in Wien.
3. Die Original-Handschrift der Partitur, im Besitz des Verlags N. Simrock in Berlin.

Die Simrocksche Partitur, 1874 erschienen, ist, von unwesentlichen Flüchtigkeiten abgesehen, fehlerfrei. Zu Beginn der 1. Variation wurde in der Pauke *p* hinzugesetzt (in Analogie mit den übrigen Stimmen). Takt 9 und 10 der 3. Variation stehen, auch in der Original-Handschrift, die Fagotte eine Terz zu tief (augenscheinlich ein Schlüsselversehen). Erwähnenswert ist, daß das Thema, wie in der Original-Handschrift sichtbar, ursprünglich für Streicher gesetzt war. Auf der ersten Seite des Autographs steht die Anmerkung: ›Das Kontrafagott ist nöthigenfalls (jedoch nur im Thema und im Finale) nach beiliegender Stimme durch eine Tuba zu ersetzen.‹

Hans Gál.

Academic Festival Overture
Op. 80

Tragic Overture

Op. 81